GOD DOESN'T RUST

Wesley T. Runk

GOD DOESN'T RUST

ISBN 0-89536-316-X

PRINTED IN U.S.A.

TABLE OF CONTENTS

A WARNING

Matthew 2:1-12, vs. 12: But when they returned to their own land, they didn't go through Jerusalem to report to Herod, for God had warned them in a dream to go home another way.

Object: A blindfold and a whistle.

Good morning, boys and girls. How many of you like to play games that use blindfolds? I want to choose a volunteer this morning who likes to wear a blindfold and who is also very good at listening [Select a volunteer.] You are sure that you are a good listener? This is what you must do. I am going to blindfold you and then I want you to walk from one side of the church to the other. You are not allowed to use your hands to feel anything and you must get there without bumping into anything. I will have the rest of the children stand at different places along the way and you are not to bump into them either. The way that you will keep from bumping into them is by listening to me. I will blow a whistle whenever I think that you might bump into anything. If you listen to me and my whistle you will get there safely. I will blow once for you to stop, twice for you to go to the left, and three times for you to go to the right. [Blindfold the volunteer and then place the other children. Let him begin his walk.]

That was very good. Listening to the one who sent you is very important. If you want to be a leader you must first learn how to take directions. Now I must tell you why I wanted you to learn the lesson of listening. A long time ago there were three men whom we remember as the wise men. They had followed a star that God had put in the heavens until it brought them to the baby Jesus. We all know how they brought fine gifts to the baby. Did you also know that they stopped in Jerusalem before they went to Bethlehem and visited with King Herod? When King Herod found out what they were doing he became very jealous. Herod thought that this child was going to take his crown, so he told the wise men in a sweet voice to stop back on their way home and tell him what they found and all about the baby King. His voice was sweet, but his heart was filled with hate. He was trying to trick the wise men.

The wise men went on following the star until they came to the manger where the baby Jesus had been born and they worshiped him. They also listened to God who had led them by the star. God warned them not to go back the way they had come but instead to go a different way. They did what the warning said, and Jesus was safe from Herod's anger. The wise men listened to the warning just as you listened to my whistle warning and the results were good. God warns us in love, and we must listen to his warnings just as we listen to his other teachings of love.

WHO WILL HE BE?

Luke 3: 15-17, 21-22, vs. 15: Everyone was expecting the Messiah to come soon, and eager to know whether or not John was he. This was the question of the hour, and was being discussed everywhere.

Object: *Pictures of pretty girls on a posterboard representing candidates for a beauty contest.*

Good morning, boys and girls. Today we are going to pretend that we are waiting for a big decision to be made. When the decision is made there will be an announcement of a winner. Have you ever had to wait for such a moment when someone would tell you what the result of a decision was, and who won? If you haven't had the experience then join with me now and find out what it is like.

I have here a big board with some pictures of the most beautiful women in the world. In a few minutes we are going to announce which one has been chosen as the most beautiful. They have to have special talents which lift one of them above the others. [*Begin to describe how one of them is a wonderful cook and how another one of them volunteers her time to take care of orphan children while another spends all her time raising money for hospitals, etc.*] These are the very special women who are both beautiful and talented. In a moment you are going to be the judge of which one is selected as out Most Talented and Beautiful Woman in the World. Now I am going to ask you to talk it over and see which one you think should get the vote. You can tell each other why you are voting for one or the other. [*Allow a few minutes for discussion.*]

Now while you are thinking about your choice, let me tell you about something like this a long time ago. It wasn't a beauty contest. Instead there was a lot of talk about different people being the Messiah, the promised one of God. Some people thought that this man might be the one while others thought it could be someone else. There were some people who thought that it could be John the Baptizer. He seemed to be the favorite of most since he talked in a way that they thought a man sent from God would talk. He was a little strange, wore different clothes, and he baptized people and made them say how sorry they were for their sins and promise not to repeat them. But John said that he wasn't the Messiah. He was not the one, but he knew who it was and this person was going to baptize with the Holy Spirit and not just with water. One day Jesus asked John to baptize him as a sign of a new time, and while John was shy about doing it at first, he did so because Jesus asked him to. All the people wondered who the Messiah was until John showed them that the real promised one of God was Jesus.

Now we can select our favorite candidate. This will remind us of the day that the people talked about who the Messiah was to be, and how John pointed the way to Jesus.

A SPECIAL TALENT

John 2:1-11, vs. 11: This miracle at Cana in Galilee was Jesus' first public demonstration of his heaven-sent power. And his disciples believed that he really was the Messiah.

Object: Choose some people in the congregation who have a special talent.

Good morning, boys and girls. Did you know that we have some very special people in our congregation who have very special talents? If I were to tell you that we have a painter in our congregation, would you be able to tell me who that person is? [*Let them answer.*] If I told you that there was someone in the church who has won a prize for her cooking, would you be able to tell me who that person is? [*Let them answer.*] Did you know that we have someone in our congregation who plays the flute with real excellence? Would you be able to tell me who that is? [*Let them answer.*] You don't know who any of these people are, and yet they all have special talents. I want to show you the painting, the special recipe, and the flute, but more than that, I want to show you the people who make these things special. [*Introduce the members who have the talents.*] Now most people do not know that these three friends have such special talents because they don't like to brag and they do these things for their own enjoyment. But from now on everyone in this church is going to know that they have these talents and they will be respected because of them. They are now known as artists, cooks, and musicians.

The reason I told you this is because I want you to know something about Jesus. There was a time when no one knew of his special power to heal, teach, or change people's lives. They thought that he was a good man with a lot of personality, but no one guessed that he was the Son of God. Then one day he was invited to a wedding with his friends and his family. After the wedding there was a reception and everyone had a lovely time. Jesus really enjoyed himself. It was a sad thing, then, when Jesus' mother came to him and said that they were running out of wine for the guests. She asked him to do something about it. Jesus was not certain what he thought his mother wanted him to do, but he did what he could. He took six jars of water and turned them into wine. It was a miracle! No one else could do it, and when the disciples saw what happened they were amazed. They believed. They knew that no ordinary man could change water into wine. This meant that Jesus was really special. From that time on people believed that he was the Son of God. This was the first time that he did something like this in public, and just as our members here this morning have revealed their special talents, no one who saw what Jesus did would ever be able to forget it.

MAKING THINGS COME TRUE

Luke 4:14-21, vs. 21:Then he added, "These Scriptures came true today!"

Object: A baby. [Ask a family of the congregation if they will share in your story today by bringing the baby forward during the sermonette.]
Good morning, boys and girls. I have a real treat for you today. I have asked one of our families if they would come forward and share with you their greatest treasure. [Ask the family to come forward.] The treasure that they have is their baby, whose name is .... Now the point that I want to make with you this morning is that from the time they planned to be married they looked forward to the time that they would have a child. A baby grows up to be a person like you and someday, after a lot more years, someone like your mom and dad and me. But when the baby is born it is special because it means that their marriage is fulfilled. In the love that they have for one another they have also given a new life which they love as much as they love one another. When the baby is born they say to themselves that their marriage has been fulfilled. This makes everything that they ever dreamed about come true.

Making things come true was an aim of Jesus. For years and years people had talked about the time that God would send the Messiah into the world. This Messiah would be the answer to everyone's dreams because it would mean that God was working with them and for them to make sure that they would be together again as one family. When Jesus came into the world it was the beginning of that hope, but many of the people did not realize it.

One day Jesus went back to his home town where people remembered him and thought of him as a very good and wise young man. Jesus went to church there.

They asked him to read the scriptures and to preach if he would like to. Jesus was asked to do this in many of the places he visited because he was very wise about the ways of God. Jesus read the scriptures and when he was finished reading he sat down. Everyone was waiting to hear what he had to say about the words that he had read. It was very quiet and then Jesus said that what he had read had come true that day. He had read about the coming of the Messiah, and when the people heard that Jesus said the words had come true there was no doubt in their minds that Jesus meant that he was the Messiah that they had waited so long for and had prayed for every day of their lives.

Jesus made it come true just as the baby made the dream come true for our friends. It is a fulfillment that has been the most important fulfillment the world has ever known. The coming of Jesus made the scripture come true and it is something that you and I will always remember and be thankful for.

SOMEONE VERY SPECIAL

Luke 4:21-30, vs. 24: But I solemnly declare to you that no prophet is accepted in his own home town.

Object: The clothes that each child wears to church that day.

Good morning, boys and girls. Today we are going to try a little experiment with each other. I think you will find it very interesting and it will help you learn something about yourself. I want you to look around while I am talking and pick out your favorite pair of shoes, your favorite sweater and your favorite dress or shirt that someone else is wearing. I want you to take a good look, because in a moment I am going to ask each of you one question. You are going to tell me which one of the things that you see someone else wearing you like the best. All of us have favorite things and they become special to us because of our feelings. I hope that all you have made your choice by now so that when I ask you to tell me which pair of shoes you would like or which sweater you like the best you can tell me. [*Begin to go around and ask the children one question about their favorite.*] I notice that all of you have chosen another person's sweater or shoes or dress. None of you said that you like your own pair of shoes the best. Have you ever noticed that we all think that the other person has the special thing that we would like? That is the way we are. I have noticed that I always think that other people have the kind of clothes, or car, or house, that I would like to have, unless what I have is brand new and it is the first time that I am using it. The other person always looks like he has the special things.

Jesus knew about this and, as a matter of fact, he told the people in his home town that this was the reason they did not think he was special. Jesus had that problem. Could you believe that some people did not think that Jesus was special? The people of Nazareth did not because they said that he was the son of Joseph and Mary. They knew him as a little boy and as he was growing up. They did not think that the same Jesus whom they had known for so long could be a prophet, or the Son of God. Jesus said that a prophet is never accepted in his home town. It was for Jesus just as it is for your clothes. People who saw Jesus said that he could not be special because he belonged to them. Sometimes you don't think your clothes are special because they belong to you.

But I know that the people later on wished they had not felt this way toward Jesus or treated him the way they did, because it was their loss not to know him as the Son of God. I hope you remember Jesus as someone very special, the most special person in the world, and you will remember this every time you thank God for the clothes that he has blessed you with. How many of you will remember Jesus as someone very special? That's wonderful.

THE REAL JEWEL

Luke 5:1-11, vs. 8: When Simon Peter realized what had happened, he fell to his knees before Jesus and said, "Oh, sir, please leave us — I'm too much of a sinner for you to have around."

Object: A diamond and some play jewelry.

Good morning, boys and girls. What do you think it would be like to be in the presence of Jesus? I wonder a lot of times what it would be like to walk or fish or just sit down in a grassy spot and talk with Jesus. There were a lot of people who had that opportunity when Jesus lived on earth, and I'm sure they loved it. It would have been wonderful to have heard his voice, touched his hand, watched him heal a sick person or preach a sermon. Jesus was so good that it would have made you shiver all over just from being near him. I remember how Peter felt sometimes when he was near Jesus. We have all heard the story about the time Jesus told the fishermen to put their nets down on the other side of the boat, and, when they did so many fish filled their nets that the boat almost sank. When Peter saw what happened he fell to his knees and asked Jesus to leave them for he thought that Jesus was too good for them.

I think I know how Peter felt. Let me show you what I mean. I have some jewelry with me this morning that I have seen lots of little girls wearing and playing with. I think that it is sort of pretty, don't you? You can buy this kind of jewelry at a discount store. Now I am going to show you a real diamond, and when you see it you will be able to tell the difference. Do you see what I mean? When you put the two kinds of jewelry together you know which is the really good kind and which is not so good. That is the way Peter felt when he stood beside Jesus. It was not the way Jesus wanted Peter to feel, but

Jesus was so good and so holy that no matter how good Peter was he would always feel like a piece of discount store jewelry and Jesus would always look like the real diamond.

There is a difference, and you and I should know that there is a difference, between God and people. It is good to know that God is that different because then we know that his love is so different that he cannot only forgive us but also bring us into his world of goodness and beauty.

The next time you see a piece of jewelry that looks like the discount store kind, you can remember what the difference is. Then when you see a real diamond, you will also remember how Peter felt when he stood beside Jesus and watched him work.

ICE CUBES

Luke 6:17-26, vs. 23: "When that happens, rejoice! Yes, leap for joy! For you will have a great reward awaiting you in heaven. And you will be in good company — the ancient prophets were treated that way too!"

Object: Some ice cubes.

Good morning, boys and girls. Today I am going to try to help you understand some of the teachings of Jesus more completely. In order to do this I will need at least one volunteer, and if there is anyone else who would like to help us he or she can come up front, too. I brought some ice cubes that I want you to hold in your hands for as long as you are able. [*Hand to the volunteers some ice cubes.*] That doesn't seem too bad, does it? As a matter of fact if feels kind of good at first, don't you think? There is a small problem though that grows into a very big problem, and I wonder if you know what I am talking about? [*Watch the children until they start to move the ice from one hand to another.*] I think you know what the problem is, don't you? That's right, the ice becomes too cold to hold in your hands. It may not seem that way at first, but in a few seconds you know that ice is too cold to handle with your bare hands.

The reason I have tried to show you this is because I want to point out that doing one thing produces another result. Cold ice makes cold hands.

Now the same thing is true about the way we live, and what we believe. Jesus tells us that Christians who live the way he teaches will have a good result or a great reward. This means that all Christians who live the good life here on earth, no matter what others try to get you to do, will have all the good things that they ever dreamed of in heaven. It may not be easy to be a

Christian today, but when the time comes for you to live with God you will know that everything here was worth it.

Living a good life and being close to God produces a great reward. Just as holding ice produces cold hands. Something done right now will make things even better later on.

That is why what you do now and what you believe now is so important. It will have a lot to do with your future with God. Jesus knew how important it was for us to lead a good life now, and he taught it to all his followers.

The next time you hold some ice in your hands or your mouth I want you to think about how your life today is important to your life with God forever.

A BRIGHT LIGHT

Luke 9:28-36, vs. 29: And as he was praying, his face began to shine, and his clothes became dazzling white and blazed with the light.

Object: A silver tray and a bright light [floodlight, if possible].

Good morning, boys and girls. How many of you have ever heard of the Mount of Transfiguration, or just the word *transfiguration?* Not very many of you. I want to tell you a story about Jesus and his disciples that I think is important for you to know and remember. There was a time when Jesus took three of his disciples up a mountain to pray and to listen to what God might have to say to them. As Jesus began to pray, something amazing happened that the disciples never forgot. I want to show you a little bit of what it might have been.

I have a silver tray that I think is beautiful. Would you agree that this is one of the prettiest trays that you have ever seen? I want to imagine for a moment that this tray is Jesus. Jesus was a beautiful person, and people liked to be around him because he made them feel beautiful also. The disciples never got used to being around Jesus because he was so beautiful. He was special, extra special. Now I am going to add something to this tray. It is a light, a bright light, and I want you to look at the tray. It shines even more brilliantly than it did before. You notice that this light does not come from inside the tray, but from the outside. It makes the tray even more beautiful. I want you to think of this light as being from Jesus' Father in Heaven.

This is what happened on Transfiguration Day. Jesus was praying and listening. All at once he started to grow brighter and brighter. He grew so bright that the disciples had to shadow their eyes when they looked at him. Not only that, but there were two men present who had died many years before. I know that you will remember their names when I tell you that they were Moses and Elijah. These two messengers of God came to tell Jesus about the plan that God had for him and they wanted Jesus to hear it and share it with his closest followers. Then it even became brighter as a cloud passed over them and a voice spoke and said, "This is my Son, my Chosen One; listen to him." Do you think that you could ever forget such an experience? The disciples couldn't and neither would we.

I wonder if you will remember Transfiguration Day the next time you see a silver tray reflect a brilliant light? I hope you will, for it is one of the great experiences of Jesus and the disciples for you to remember.

STUPID TESTS FOR GOD

Luke 4:1-13, vs. 12: Jesus replied, "The Scriptures also say, 'Do not put the Lord your God to a foolish test.'"

Object: A toy gun [hand pistol which has a barrel that moves].

Good morning, boys and girls. Today I am going to show you something that I think is stupid. Did you ever think that you would come to church and hear the pastor tell you that he was going to show you something that was stupid? I didn't think either that I would do this, but I am going to with the hope that you will learn something very important. I brought with me a toy gun. Toy guns are not my favorite toys. I wish that people would stop making guns and shooting them, and then maybe we would stop making toy guns. Nevertheless it will teach us something important about how we should act toward God.

How many of you have ever heard of Russian roulette? [*Let them answer.*] Some of you have heard of that very foolish game. In Russian roulette a person takes the gun and puts one bullet in it. Then he takes the barrel of the gun and spins it so that he doesn't have any idea where the bullet is in the gun. Now he is betting that the gun will not go off when he fires it. But to even make this game more foolish he holds the gun to his head and pulls the trigger. If he is lucky the one bullet is somewhere else in the gun; but if he is not, then he dies. This is called a test of luck. I call that foolish and stupid.

Some people put God to that kind of test and Jesus says that is it foolish. The Devil is always trying to get people to put God to that kind of a test. The Devil tried to get Jesus to test God in a foolish way by having Jesus jump off the tallest building in town with the hope that God would send angels to catch him before he hit the ground. Jesus told the Devil that this was a stupid way to try to show God's power and love. Jesus would not test God in foolish ways.

Playing Russian roulette is one of the ways some people think that they are testing God. If God is on their side, they reason, the gun will not go off while they are holding it to their head. Boys and girls dare one another to do stupid things to see if the other one is brave. If you accept such a stupid dare with the hope that God will save you, then you are going to be disappointed because God does not jump to answer our foolish tests.

I am sure that Jesus told us about this so that we would always remember not to make up foolish tests for God. Instead we should trust God and do what is reasonable and loving to and for each other.

A RIDDLE

Luke 13:31-35, vs. 34: "O Jerusalem, Jerusalem! The city that murders prophets. The city that stones those sent to help her. How often I have wanted to gather your children together even as a hen protects her brood under her wings, but you wouldn't let me."

Object: Some rubber boots, a band aid, and a baseball glove.

Good morning, boys and girls. How many of you like to play riddles if the riddles are not too difficult? Oh, that's good. I like riddles, but I don't like them if they are so hard that I cannot get them after a few guesses. Here is my riddle. How are some rubber boots [*hold them up*], a band aid [*hold it up*], and a baseball glove [*hold it up*] alike? Do you think that you can guess that riddle? Somehow or other they all do the same thing. Can you guess what it is? [*Let them guess.*] They all protect something else from being hurt. Your boots keep your shoes from getting wet and being damaged, the band aid protects a cut from getting infected, and the baseball glove keeps your hands from being hurt when you catch a ball that is thrown hard. All of these things protect you.

Jesus is also a protector of people who want his protection. He used to tell the people of Jerusalem that he would like to protect them from all of the hurt and trouble that was coming their way. He knew how trouble followed where people taught the wrong things about God. Jesus wanted to help people do the right thing so that they would not get hurt, but many people would not listen. Instead they decided to do things their own way and a lot of times they got hurt or they caused someone else to get hurt. Jesus said there was a way to live and be happy and protected against all of the bad things in the world, but that they would have to follow his teachings.

That is why Jesus is like a band aid, baseball glove, or a pair of rubber boots. He also wants to protect us from the devil and all of the devil's friends.

The next time you see a band aid, a pair of rubber boots, or even a baseball glove, I hope that you will think about the way Jesus wants to protect us from the things that are wrong in the world.

A BULLDOZER IN YOUR LIFE

Luke 13:1-9, vs. 8: '"Give it one more chance,' the gardener answered. 'Leave it another year, and I'll give it special attention and plenty of fertilizer. If we get figs next year, fine; if not, I'll cut it down.'"

Object: A toy bulldozer.

Good morning, boys and girls. How many times have you wished that you could start over on some project? Have you ever wished that you could draw that certain picture over, or start the game again after you made the wrong move, or something else like that? I know you have. I have watched people start over on things for as long as I can remember. There are big machines that do nothing but tear down buildings that are no good anymore, or had too many mistakes when they were built the first time.

I brought along a toy bulldozer because it is a symbol of destroying things that are in the way, or that are old, or mistakes that have been made. How many of you have seen a bulldozer push over a building that needed to be torn down? I knew that you had seen this happen.

Sometimes we need something like a bulldozer in our lives to make the kind of changes that God wants us to make. Do you know what I mean? Suppose God gave a life and the life that he made did nothing but just kind of stand around and do nothing. Don't you think that God would like to give that life a push and change it around so that it would start doing something right? I do. Or how about the person who does something wrong and harmful not only to himself, but also to others. Don't you think that God wishes that he could bulldoze that life in such a way that it would change and start doing things right?

I know that he feels a little bit like this because Jesus talked about how God felt when he saw one of his fruit trees that did not produce good fruit. He thought that such a tree should be cut down and another tree put in its place.

The thing for us to remember is that God is not happy or satisfied with wrong lives. He wants wrong lives to change and be made better. We do not want a town of old buildings that are not used or trees that do not grow. We want those things changed. The same is true about the way God feels about our lives. He wants us to change the bad and make even better what is already good. The next time you see a bulldozer changing things, maybe you will remember the things that you have done wrong and you will change them.

SHOES ON THE WRONG FEET

Luke 15:1-32, vs. 17: "When he finally came to his senses, he said to himself, 'At home even the hired men have food enough to spare, and here I am, dying of hunger.'"

Object: Have the children reverse their shoes: right shoe on left foot, left shoe on right foot.

Good morning, boys and girls. Have you ever put your shoes on the wrong feet and then walked so long that your feet began to hurt? I want you to do that for me. Take your shoes off and put them on the wrong feet and then just stand up while I am talking to you about the story for this morning. [*Let them all change their shoes at this point.*] The reason I am doing this will be shown to you as you hear what I have to say.

You see, sometimes we do things the wrong way, but it seems right to us or we are too stubborn to admit that we are wrong. Jesus told a story about a young man who wanted to get away from his family and spend some of the money that he knew would be his when his father died. He was too young to know how to take care of a lot of money, but he wanted the money anyway. His father didn't want him to go, but he could not talk him out of it. The young man went away and for a short time he had a ball. He spent money doing all the things that he knew were wrong. As I said, at first it seemed like a lot of fun even though it was wrong. But after a while the money was spent and he was sick and finally he noticed that even the pigs were eating better than he was.

What do you do when that happens? It is like having your shoes on backward. At first it seems like some fun. It is different, and who knows, maybe that is the way it should be. But after a while they begin to hurt. What do you do? I'll tell you what the young man did. He came to his senses and decided to change it all by going back to his father and telling him how wrong it was for him to act the way that he did, and that he was sorry for it. The Bible says that he came to his senses. Jesus told that story so that we would know that God our Father is always ready to forgive us for whatever sin we have committed if we are sorry and change our ways.

Wearing your shoes on the wrong feet is a foolish thing to do because it not only hurts your feet but it also ruins your shoes. Some people will not change even if it hurts because they want people to think that they did it on purpose and they like it that way. Some people keep on sinning because they are afraid to admit that they are wrong. But for those who do admit they are wrong and want to change, God forgives them. Then they start over fresh. Whenever you see your shoes and put them on the right feet think how great it is to be right with God.

SALT IN THE COFFEE

Luke 20:9-19, vs. 17: Jesus looked at them and said, "Then what does the Scripture mean where it says, 'The Stone rejected by the builders was made the cornerstone'?"

Object: Some salt for coffee and some pencil lead for a ball point pen.

Good morning, boys and girls. Have you ever noticed how people want to do things their own way even if it is not right? Some people will try to make something fit into a box that is too small, or they will try to tell you that the moon is made of cheese and they want you to believe that. I brought along some things that I have seen people do wrong and would not admit it. Let me try this first. I saw a man put salt into his coffee thinking that it was sugar. Even though he did it wrong he was afraid to admit that he made a mistake, so he drank it that way even though it tasted terrible. Here is another one. I saw some boys the other day trying to put pencil lead into a ball point pen thinking that they could make the pen write again. When I told them they needed an ink refill they told me that they had done it this way before and it worked, so they knew that it would work this time. I knew that it didn't, and so did they, but they would never let me know that this would not work in a thousand years. They were just like the man with salt in his coffee.

Some people are like that about believing in Jesus. They know that they need help, that they need a God such as Jesus spoke about, and yet they will not give it a try. Instead they will look for every other way out of their mess, except trying to go with God. Jesus is the only way to happiness and a good life, but people will try everything else before they will try him. Jesus talked about the way that men will even kill him before they will do it his way. They cannot stand his goodness or his love, so they call him names and lie about what he said and did, and finally they will talk people into killing him thinking that they are doing a favor for God. They will not admit that they are wrong.

What Jesus said would happen did happen. Men DID lie and cheat and finally murder him, but God still had the last word. They could not kill Jesus. Instead he came back to life and lives forever. God is able to overcome everything that is wrong and make it right.

If you are trying to live without God, you are like the man who put salt in his coffee and would not admit that he had made a mistake. Just think how much more he would have liked that coffee with some sugar instead of salt. You will enjoy life a lot more when you have Jesus in your life than you ever did without him.

CHEERS FOR JESUS

Luke 19:28-40, vs. 40: "If they keep quiet, the stones along the road will burst into cheers."

Object: Some stones of various shapes and sizes.

Good morning, boys and girls. How many of you ever get excited? Almost all of you do. What do you do when you are excited? [*Let them answer.*] Have you ever gone to a basketball game or baseball game and gotten excited? Did you cheer, shout, scream, or yell? I know that when I go to a game and my team begins to score points, and it looks like we are going to catch the team ahead of us, or go on to win the game, I find that I am standing up and cheering my head off! I love to cheer. Do you think that you could be excited about something and not cheer? Suppose you were at a game and the team you wanted to win was doing just great but there was a rule that said that you could not cheer. Let's just try it and see what happens. First of all you must cheer. How about "Hip, hip hooray! Hip, hip, hooray!" Terrific! Let's hear you do it again. [*Let them repeat it until it seems that they are really in the mood.*] Do you like to cheer? Well, you can't! You are not allowed to cheer. From now on for the rest of the morning you are not allowed to cheer no matter how much you feel like doing it. Just think of that, here you feel like cheering, and I won't let you. It is disappointing, isn't it?

This happened to Jesus on Palm Sunday many years ago. He was coming down the very narrow streets of Jerusalem and the people, thousands of them, were standing and cheering and throwing their robes on the ground for the donkey on which Jesus was riding to walk on, and the people who were in charge were telling the others to be quiet. They thought that it was wrong for the people to call Jesus the Lord and shout praises to God. Do you know what Jesus said? He said that if the people kept quiet that the stones in the street would cheer. It was such a happy moment and the people were so thrilled about what God had done that Jesus knew that even the stones would cheer. Have you ever heard a stone cheer? Have you ever heard a stone do or say anything? Of course you haven't but Jesus knew that there was no way that you could keep people from praising God on such a happy day.

I hope that you have many days like that. I hope that you shout, praise and cheer God every day of your life. Because, you know, if you keep quiet about God, the next thing you know God may have to listen to the stones to hear a noise, and if you don't speak then maybe they will.

Will you shout praises to God? That's wonderful. So will I.

HE'S NOT IN THE CEMETERY

Luke 24:1-11, vs. 5: The women were terrified and bowed low before them. Then the men asked, "Why are you looking in a tomb for someone who is alive?"

Object: Some signs that have printed on them the words of these places: SCHOOL, RESTAURANT, GARAGE, CHURCH, CEMETERY.

Good morning, boys and girls. Today I am going to see how sharp you really are with a little game that I have devised. I have some signs that I want held up and I will need some volunteers for this part of the game. [*Pass out the signs.*] Now I am going to suggest some words and when you think of the sign that goes with the word you should go over and stand by that sign. [*Make sure that they understand what you are doing.*] The first word is EDUCATION. If you see something that reminds you of the word education then go stand by that sign. Very good. How about this word: WRECK. An automobile wreck. Where would you go with an automobile wreck? Very good. Let's try a T-BONE STEAK. Where would you like to eat your steak? In a garage? And how about SUNDAY SCHOOL and WORSHIP? So far you have found all of the right places. There is one sign left. Does anyone know what you find when you go to the CEMETERY? That's right, it is for dead people. It is the place where people are buried after they die.

If I asked you to find Jesus where would you look? Would you go to the cemetery sign or where would you go? [*Let them answer.*] Is Jesus dead? The Bible says that he was crucified on the cross and died. Do you think that you could find Jesus in a cemetery where other people are who have died?

Let me tell you a little story. Some of Jesus' closest friends were some women who felt sad about Jesus' dying and they wanted to do something about it. They went to the place that he was buried on a Sunday morning and when they arrived there, they were met by two angels who asked them what person they were looking for. They told the angels that they were looking for Jesus. They angels said that they were in the wrong place if they were looking for Jesus. Jesus is alive and well so why should he be in a grave at the cemetery? I can tell you that they were very surprised but very happy.

I know that this is the way that you feel also. You know that Jesus is not in any cemetery, but instead he is alive with his Father in Heaven and he lives with us today. That is the wonderful thing about Easter. Jesus is alive and he promises us that we will live also just as he does.

HAVE YOU READ ABOUT JESUS?

John 20:19-31, vs. 30-31: Jesus' disciples saw him do many other miracles besides the ones told about in this book, but these are recorded so that you will believe that he is the Messiah, the Son of God, and that believing in him you will have life.

Object: Some books about American history or a biographical sketch about your favorite hero.

Good morning, boys and girls. Have you ever asked yourselves why the Bible was written? Did you ever wonder if the person who wrote part of the Bible thought that someday a person like you might be reading it? It is a very interesting question. Most people would wonder about that for a long time, but I am going to tell you that I think the answer to the question is "yes." At least I know that the writer of the book of John thought that people were going to read it.

Do you think that President Kennedy thought that people would write about him and his country, the United States? I think that he knew they would, and sure enough, I have some books here to show you that the people have done a lot of writing about the man John Kennedy and the United States. Almost everything that was important has been written about and even some things that were not too important have been written down and printed in books.

Now if people would write about someone important like John Kennedy, do you think that others would write about a person they thought was the most important person who ever lived? I think so. As a matter of fact, there was a man called John who said that the very reason that he had written what he did was so that people could read about Jesus and know that he was God. Later on in his book he said that there would not be enough pages or room in the world to tell all of the things that Jesus did that proved that he was God, but that he had written down a few of the things so that we could believe. That means that John had an idea that there were some people asking questions and wanting answers that only someone who had lived and loved Jesus could give the answers to.

That is the reason the Bible was written. It is a record of some of the wonderful things that Jesus did while he was on earth. I don't know if you ever thought about reading about what God has done in the same way that you can read about John Kennedy or George Washington, but if you want to know what Jesus was really like and how God feels about certain things, you can find all of the answers in this book that we call the Bible.

How many of you want to read about the wonderful things Jesus did? I hope you all will.

THE MISSING FISH

*John 21:1-14, vs. 5: He called, "Any fish, boys?" "No,"
we replied.*

Object: Fishing pole, empty stringer, tackle box.

Good morning, boys and girls. How many of you go fishing? Do you have good luck? I mean, do you catch lots of fish when you go fishing? I know that everyone likes to think he will catch a lot of fish when he takes his pole, stringer, and tackle box to the lake or river. For some reason it doesn't work like that for me. I have everything that you should have when you go fishing, but something is missing. Fish! I have lots of bait but I don't seem to be able to catch fish. It gets pretty discouraging sometimes.

Whenever that happens I like to read one of my very favorite stories in the Bible. I want to tell you a little bit about it. It was in the evening when Peter and some of his friends decided that they would go fishing. Things hadn't been going too well for them. First it was Jesus dying, and now the same people who killed Jesus were looking for them, too, and, to be very honest, the disciples were a little afraid. They knew a night on the Sea of Galilee would help them feel better so they went fishing. Well, I want you to know that they didn't catch a fish all night. Were they discouraged! Here they were, some of the best fishermen in the world, and they couldn't catch fish. That part always makes me feel kind of good.

It was almost morning and just starting to get light when one of the disciples heard a voice from shore shouting to them. It was kind of hard to make out for sure who it was, but the person was asking if they had caught any fish. People aways like to ask other fishermen what kind of fish they have caught and how many. The disciples called back that they hadn't had a bite. "Well, put your net on the other side," the man on the beach said, and they did. You guessed it! There were so many fish the boat wouldn't hold them. The voice told them to come in for breakfast and share their joy. Now the disciples knew what some of them had suspected. The man on the beach was Jesus. The fish didn't even matter. Peter jumped over the side and began to swim and the others brought the boat to shore as fast as they could. It was Jesus and were they glad to see him! They remembered how he looked when he was dying on the cross, but now he looked fine and he certainly was enjoying life.

I think that is one of the best stories about Jesus I ever heard. The fish were not very important once they found out that Jesus was alive and ready to start sharing himself in the way that he always had done before. He will share himself with you also if you want him to, even when you haven't caught a fish!

Will you remember this story the next time you go fishing? That's good.

RECOGNIZING THE VOICE

John 10:22-30, vs. 27: My sheep recognize my voice, and I know them, and they follow me.

Object: A tape recorder and a sound track` of the pastor's voice and some voices that the children would recognize from TV.

Good morning, boys and girls. We're going to do something this morning that I know you are going to enjoy. How many of you have ever listened to a tape recorder? [*Let them answer.*] That's good. How many of you have ever heard your own voice on the tape recorder? Did you think that your own voice sounded strange or different? Most people do, and they are surprised that their voice sounds the way it does. I have recorded some voices on this tape recorder. I am going to ask you to tell me who you think they are. Do you understand? It's kind of a game. [*Begin to play the tape and tell the children to raise their hands as they recognize the voices.*] That was very good. You know a lot of people by the sound of their voices. Let's see if you can recognize one other voice I have on the tape. [*Play your own voice.*] That's right, it is I.

Now there is a good reason why I have done this. I want you to remember this part of it when you think about the tape recorder. Jesus wanted all his followers to know and trust him. He talked about how a shepherd could speak and only his sheep would listen. When a shepherd called his sheep only his sheep would follow him. The sheep knew the shepherd's voice, and they trusted the shepherd so they followed him. Voices that we know and trust are good voices. Jesus did not just want to be great or strong or handsome. Jesus wants to be trusted and loved. That was the most important thing to him and he worked at it with all of his strength.

That's what Jesus meant when he talked about the sheep recognizing the voice of the shepherd. The sheep trusted their leader. So Jesus says the people who believe in God should listen to him because he also can be trusted to do the right thing for all of his followers. We are followers of Jesus and we trust him to do everything that is right for us.

When you see a tape recorder and listen to voices that you recognize, then you will also think about how Jesus taught that we should listen to the teachings of God and trust in Jesus, just as the sheep listened to the shepherd and trusted in him.

A YARDSTICK FOR BELIEVERS

John 13:31-35, vs. 35: Your strong love for each other will prove to the world that you are my disciples.

Object: A yardstick.

Good morning, boys and girls. How many of you have ever had to prove something to someone else? Suppose you told someone that you were seven years old and he said he didn't believe you. What would you do? [*Let them answer.*] Is that proof? You could show him your birth certificate if you knew where it was, and that would prove how old you are. I have something here that helps proves things. What do you call this? [*Hold up the yardstick.*] That's right, a yardstick. What do you do with one of these? [*Let them answer.*] That means that I can prove that I am six feet tall. If I tell you that I am six feet tall and you tell me to prove it, I can measure myself. If I am two yardsticks tall, then I have proven that I am six feet tall. I can prove how long or short almost anything is with this yardstick. We will call the yardstick a prover.

There are other things to prove that are even more important. One of these important things is something that Jesus said to his disciples about being his followers. How can you prove that you are a follower of Jesus? That's important, isn't it? Jesus said that there would be a lot of people who would want to know if you were a follower or not. How do you suppose that Jesus thought you could prove it to others? [*Let them answer.*] The way that Jesus said he would prove it was by the way that you love one another. Christians love other people. You cannot hide love or pretend to love. Love is something very real, and it is the one sign that shows people how you really feel about Jesus. If you are looking for ways to help others, then you are proving that you love Jesus. If you are willing to listen to others, then you are showing your love and also the fact that you are a follower of Jesus.

Loving each other is real proof of being a follower of Jesus. It is just like a yardstick or anything else that you use to prove that something is true or not true.

This is one of the very important proofs that you will want to make every day of your life, and it is not only proof for other people, but it is also proof for yourself.

How many of you will prove that you are followers of Jesus by loving one another? Raise your hands. That's wonderful.

THE HOLY SPIRIT IS A STRING?

John 14:23-29, vs. 26: But when the Father sends the Comforter instead of me — and by the Comforter I mean the Holy Spirit — he will teach you much, as well as remind you of everything I myself have told you.

Object: A piece of string tied to your finger.

Good morning, boys and girls. How many of you ever need a reminder? I mean a real reminder, like the one I have tied around my finger? Do you know what I have tied around my finger? [Let them answer.] Yes, it's a piece of string, but do you know why that string is there? I put the string around my finger so that I would not forget to return a book to the library. I was supposed to return it several days ago and I keep forgetting, so today I tied a string around my finger so that I could not forget. Have you ever forgotten anything? What do you do to help you remember? Some people write notes to themselves, and others have even tied an onion around their necks to help them remember something very important.

Jesus told his followers that there was another kind of reminder that was more important than anything that we have ever tied around a finger or held in our hand. This reminder was the Holy Spirit. Jesus knew that before long he was going to return to Heaven and live with the Father, and he did not want all of his teachings to be forgotten. There was a plan and it was a wonderful one. Jesus told them that when he returned to heaven the Holy Spirit would come and live with every disciple and remind them of everything that Jesus taught them. It was a wonderful plan because now the disciples could go wherever Jesus wanted them to go and God would be with each one of them. Before, Jesus had to be with all twelve in the same place, but now the Spirit could be in as many places as there were believers. The Holy Spirit did not have a body and did not have to be in one place at one time. The Holy Spirit could be in many places at the same time. If Peter wanted to visit one town and John wanted to visit another and James wanted to go somewhere else, then the Holy Spirit could be with all three of them, and he could remind them every moment of what Jesus taught them and did for them. That is why Jesus called the Holy Spirit a reminder.

You have the same reminder that the disciples had because the Holy Spirit is always with you just as he was with the disciples. It is the Holy Spirit who reminds you about the teachings of Jesus, and nothing else is as good at doing it. You can tie some strings around your finger to help you remember the library book that you keep forgetting, but the Holy Spirit will remind you about Jesus and all of his teachings.

GOD — A TEA BAG, WATER, AND LEMON

John 17:20-26, vs. 21: My prayer for all of them is that they will be of one heart and mind, just as you and I are, Father — that as you are in me and I am in you, so they will be in us, and the world will believe you sent me.

Object: A tea bag, some hot water, and a slice of lemon.

Good morning, boys and girls. I have something to show you this morning that will help you to learn something about the way of God and what he wants for us. I'm sure that you have seen the things I brought, and when I get done I am hoping that you will understand how three different things can all be together like one.

First of all I have some hot water. Now I know all of you have had hot water before, but we are going to call this hot water God the Father. Can you imagine that? God the Father is hot water. The second thing that I brought is a tea bag and we are going to call the tea in the bag Jesus. So we have God the Father as hot water, Jesus as tea and just to add a little to it we are going to have a slice of lemon. We'll call the lemon the followers of Jesus. Now as you look at these three things you can see that they are all different. If I asked you to pick out the disciples, you could pick them out, couldn't you? [*Let them pick out the lemon.*] But I am going to do something with the three of them and I want you to follow me very closely. I am going to put the tea bag in a cup, pour the hot water over the tea bag, and then squeeze the lemon into the cup. I will take the tea bag out of the cup and put it away and also throw away the lemon. Now I want you to look in the cup and pick out the hot water, or the lemon, or the tea, and show it to me. Do you think that you can do it? Is there hot water in the cup? Is there lemon in the cup?

Is there tea in the cup? All three are in the cup, but you cannot pick out any one of them without picking them all out.

The reason that I wanted you to see this is so that you would understand a prayer that Jesus prayed to his **Father** in Heaven. Jesus prayed that the followers would be together with God the Father just as God the Father was with him.

All three — the Father, Jesus and the followers — are together as one. Because we are followers we are in Jesus, and Jesus is in us, and we are in God the Father, and God the Father is in us, just as the tea, lemon and hot water are all together. Isn't that tremendous that we are all one together and together we are one?

The next time you see a cup of tea you can remember how everything goes together and makes it one drink. When you do, you will also remember how God, Jesus and you and I are all together with God.

GOD'S HEATING PAD

John 15:26-27; 16:4b-11, vs. 26: But I will send you the Comforter — the Holy Spirit, the source of all truth. He will come to you from the Father and will tell you all about me.

Object: A heating pad.

Good morning, boys and girls. How many of you have you ever been sick with a real ache, like a backache or an earache or a leg ache? I see that a lot of you know what I am talking about. What do you do when you feel bad? [Let them answer.] You go to bed and take some medicine and try to sleep as much as possible. Do any of you ever use a heating pad? [Show them the heating pad.] A lot of you have used a heating pad. Doesn't that feel good on your back or your head when the ache is there? It sure does. Inside that pad are a bunch of wires that get warm when the electricity is turned on, and that is what makes us feel better. It is kind of like our mother's arms holding us and keeping us comforable. Another way of saying it is that the heating pad is a comfort to us when we are sick or hurt.

I would like to compare the heating pad to the Holy Spirit. Jesus said the Holy Spirit is a Comforter. He makes us feel better because we know that we can depend on the Holy Spirit to bring us the truth. People like you and me feel very much alone sometimes, and the Holy Spirit is a comfort to us. He lets us know that God is near and ready to talk to us in prayer. When we are hurt the Holy Spirit comforts us by speaking softly and telling us that God will heal us. Even when we grow old and we are ready to die, the Holy Spirit comforts us. He makes sure that we know that death is not a bad thing for people who love God, because God is waiting to bring us safely into his home. The Holy

Spirit comforts us with the truth, just as the heating pad comforts us with warmth when we are hurt.

A lot of us wonder who the Holy Spirit is and where we can find him, but the wonderful part about the Holy Spirit is that you don't have to hunt for him because he is here. He comforts us when we hurt, when we are afraid, and even when we are alone. That is why Jesus calls him the Comforter.

The next time you see the heating pad, maybe you will think of the word "comfort." When you think of that, then maybe you will also think of the Holy Spirit whom Jesus called the Comforter.

OUR GUIDE

John 16:12-15, vs. 13a: When the Holy Spirit, who is truth, comes, he shall guide you into all truth, for he will not be presenting his own ideas, but will be passing on to you what he has heard.

Object: A needle, some thread.

Good morning, boys and girls. Have any of you ever been lost or thought that you might be lost? [*Let them answer.*] If you haven't been lost, then have you ever been in a dark room and wished that someone would take your hand and lead you to a light? All of us have been in the dark and have needed someone to guide us or wished that someone would be able to guide us. That is what I want to talk to you about this morning.

I brought with me an excellent guide, one of the best I know [*Hold up the needle*]. How many of you have ever seen or used a needle? Good, all of you know something about a needle. A needle is a guide for the thread. The thread follows the needle wherever it goes. If you want to sew a button on a shirt or a coat, you take the needle and put it through the holes in the button and it will lead the thread right through to the shirt or coat. If you want to come back the thread will follow the needle through the same hole that way also. The needle is an excellent guide. If the needle can't get through, then the thread will not be able to go there either.

That is something that we learn about the Holy Spirit. The Holy Spirit is a guide, a true guide. Wherever the Holy Spirit leads us, we know that we can follow. We also know that we have nothing to be afraid of if the Holy Spirit is our guide. Jesus said that the Spirit is truth and teaches truth. If we learn something from the Holy Spirit we know that it is the truth. If the Spirit guides us like the needle, and we follow like the thread, then we will have no problems wherever he goes we are welcomed and trusted.

Now we have learned two things about the Holy Spirit that are really important. We know that he is a comfort, and we know that he is a guide. I hope that the next time you see a needle it will remind you of the Holy Spirit, and that when you think of him, you will also remember that he is a guide you can trust.

AUTHORITY

Luke 7:10, vss. 7,8: Just speak a word from where you are, and my servant boy will be healed! I know, because I am under the authority of my superior officers, and I have authority over my men.

Object: Some signs of authority like "Keep Out" or "No Parking."

Good morning, boys and girls. Do you ever read the signs in yards or on buildings when you take a drive? Some of them are very interesting and some of them are very demanding. The interesting ones are usually funny or pretty, but the ones that speak like a command are the ones that I would like to talk about today. How many of you have seen a sign like this: "Keep Out" or "Keep Off The Grass?" You don't have to ask anyone what that means, do you? You know that the sign means exactly what it says. It speaks with authority. the sign almost sounds like [*Say this with a very commanding voice.*] KEEP OUT or KEEP OFF THE GRASS. That is pretty impressive. Have you ever seen your mom or dad somewhere where the sign says "No Parking"? If they do, they run wherever they have to go, or if they stay in the car, they keep the motor running. No one feels too good about parking where the sign says "No Parking."

The reason for that is that someone with authority put up those signs. It may have been the person who lives in the house who has the right to protect his property. Or it may have been a policeman who put up the sign. Whoever put up the sign has authority, and that is what I want to talk to you about.

Authority is important, and not everybody has it about everything except one: God has authority. When God wants something done it is done, and when he speaks it is a command. The gospel lesson for today talks about when Jesus healed a slave who belonged to a man in the army. The man in the army knew that when Jesus spoke it was with authority, and that meant that it would happen. The army man knew that Jesus did not have to be in a certain place or touch the sick slave for the slave to get well. All Jesus had to do was say it, and it was done.

That is real authority. It is something for us to remember about God. When God speaks it is with authority, and while he doesn't yell or put up signs, he still means what he says and what he says gets done. God has authority and he uses his authority all the time.

HOW WE CARE

Luke 7:11-17, vs. 13: When the Lord saw her, his heart overflowed with sympathy, "Don't cry!' he said.

Object: Some flowers, and some greeting cards.

Good morning, boys and girls. Today I want to tell you something that I think is really important to know about God, and how I know that it is true. Did you know that God really cares about us? Did you know that God feels sorry when we hurt, or are disappointed? Did you know that? What do we do when someone we like very much has to go to the hospital to be operated on? What do we do when a friend of ours has someone very close to him die? Do you know what we do? [*Let them answer.*]

I have some of the things that people send their friends who go into the hospital. [*Take out the greeting card and the vase of flowers or the planter.*] This is one way that people have of showing that they care, and that they are thinking about the person who is ill. We do the same kind of things when someone dies. We send cards or flowers or we give money to places like the church or cancer fund in the name of the person who died, with the hope that it will help someone else. The reason we do things like this is to show people that we care.

Jesus cared a lot about people when they were sick and when they lost a loved one. Our lesson for today talks about one time when Jesus saw a woman crying because her only child, a young man, had died. Jesus knew how much the woman loved her son, and that she had no one else at home because her husband had already died. The Bible says that Jesus' heart overflowed with caring and he said to the woman, "Don't cry." It really would be enough to know that Jesus cared, but he didn't stop there. This is one of those times when Jesus did a miracle. He went over to the casket and looked inside where the young man lay dead. He told him to wake up and come back to life. Jesus knew how hard it was for that woman to be all alone, so he cared enough to bring her son back to life.

It is good to know that God cares that much about us and how we feel when we are sad. That is why I know that he cares about me today, and that he cares about you also. The next time you show someone how much you care by sending him a card or some flowers, I want you to think about how much Jesus cares for people also, and how much he cares for you. When you think about it, you will find that you feel good all over.

A MATCH IS FOR BURNING

Luke 7:36-50, vs. 47: Therefore her sins — and they are many — are forgiven for she loved me much; but one who is forgiven little shows little love.

Object: Some wooden matches.

Good morning, boys and girls. Have you ever known anyone who thought he never did anything wrong? No matter what happens he is always right, and the other person is wrong. I can tell that you all know someone like that. I hope that you are not that way, but that's what I am going to talk about today.

These people think they are perfect, and they look a little bit like this match that I am showing you right now. [*Hold up a fresh wooden match.*] Do you see how it is made? Just perfect. It has a beautiful blue head and a very straight stick. We can't find much fault with it. Now I want to show you another match. Look at it [*Hold up a stub of a wooden match that has been burned.*] Do you know what is wrong with this match? That's right, it has been burned. It has been used. It gave light, fire, heat for someone else. That is what a match is for, and that is the way any good match should really look.

Jesus tells us about people who are just like these matches. He knew some people who thought they never did anything wrong. They were so good that they never thought to love anyone else. They looked perfect. They were always clean, they dressed just right, and they ate only the best food. They were really something. They watched everything they said so that other people would never think bad about them. They also thought that God owed them a favor, and they never asked God to forgive them because they never thought that they did anything wrong.

They looked the same way when they died as they did when they were born. They were clean and smooth.

But there were other types of people. For instance, there was a woman whom he knew who did some awful things and got into a lot of trouble, but she knew that she was wrong and asked God to forgive her. She didn't worry about the things that she had done wrong, but she asked how she could help others whom she had hurt. She loved God, and when she did wrong she told him. Jesus loved that woman a lot more than the man who thought that he did nothing wrong. She was like a burned-up match. She used herself to help others and to love God. She gave light to people who lived in the dark, and love to those whom other people hated. God loves people like that woman.

I hope that you know when you are wrong and tell God about it, and that you share yourselves like my burned-up match. That is the way God gets close to us and shares himself with us.

BREAD IS FOR EATING

Luke 9:18-24, vs. 24: Whoever loses his life for my sake will save it, but whoever insists on keeping his life will lose it.

Object: A piece of stale bread.

Good morning, boys and girls. How many of you like to eat bread, really good bread? I do, too. Good bread is one of the real joys of life. How many of you like it hot and dripping with butter and jam? I like that, too. Sometimes I like my bread so much that I try to save it and save it. Do you know what happens to good bread when you try to save it for a long time? [*Let them answer.*] That's right, it gets stale. It also molds and turns gray and green. Is there anyone here who likes gray, green stale bread? No one? Not one of you likes that kind of bread. Then why do we save it? [*Let them answer.*] There is no real reason, because bread is meant to be used and eaten. When you eat and use the bread it does several good things. For one thing, it tastes good when it is eaten. It also turns into body cells and makes us grow and be strong. That is the way bread was meant to be. It should be used and not saved.

It is the same way with living. A life that is used is a good life. A life that is protected and saved is no good. Jesus taught us a long time ago that we should stop worrying about our lives, and that we should use them to do good, and to work for God. Some people are afraid to be Christians and to follow Jesus. It sounds dangerous and they are afraid that he will ask too much from them. They want to save their lives for other things they think are important for them. But whenever you save your lives, you lose them just as you lose the bread by saving it.

Jesus wants us to spend our lives, use them and work for him and he promises us that whatever we give to him will be made into something better. When you eat bread you don't become bread. You become a body. When you work for Jesus and give your life to him, you become something even better. That is a promise of Jesus, and Jesus always keeps his promises. So don't save your life for something that you might think will be important. Give your life to Jesus now and you will be glad that you did.

DID JESUS HAVE A HOUSE?

Luke 9:51-62, vs. 58: But Jesus replied, "Remember, I don't even own a place to lay my head. Foxes have dens to live in, and birds have nests, but I, the Messiah, have no earthly home at all."

Object: A bird house, dog house, or fish bowl.

Good morning, boys and girls. Have you ever wondered about where Jesus lived? Do you know where he lived? Was it a big house or a small house? Was it made of stone, or mud, or wood? How many rooms did it have, and who were his neighbors? Does anyone know the answer to those questions? When Jesus was a little boy, he lived with his father and mother in a house, but when he grew up and started his ministry to people, the Bible tells us that Jesus did not have a home that he could call his own. That is kind of strange, isn't it?

Look what I have, and then maybe you will understand how different Jesus was compared to you and me. Do you live in a house? Of course you do. I have some other kinds of houses to show you how important a house is to everyone. [*Hold up the bird house.*] Who lives in this house? That's right, birds. Do all birds live in houses like this? Where do the others live? That's right, in a nest. [*Hold up the fish bowl and ask the same questions.*] Even the fish have a place to stay. It seems odd that everyone has a place to stay except Jesus. But Jesus had a very good reason for not wanting a house. Let's see if you can guess why Jesus did not have a house.

If you have a house, you must always come home to the same people. Jesus wanted to be with all the people he could while he was here on earth. Jesus wanted to share himself with everyone and use all of his time to teach and preach and heal the sick.

Suppose he had to cut the grass or paint the house or cook meals. It would have kept him from meeting all the people he wanted to. Jesus was a person who needed to keep moving if the world was going to know God's plan, and he could not worry about a home to take care of while he lived here on earth. God doesn't mind us having houses, or the birds or fish having homes, but Jesus had the most important work that God ever gave to anyone, and he could not let anything take away from the time he had to do it.

When you think about your home, or when you go home today, I want you to look around and thank God for sharing Jesus with us and making us first on his list and the house second.

DOMINOES DOWN!

Luke 10:1-9, 16, vs. 16: Then he said to the disciples, "Those who welcome you are welcoming me. And those who reject you are rejecting me. And those who reject me are rejecting God who sent me.

Object: Some dominoes.

Good morning, boys and girls. How many of you have ever played with dominoes? It used to be a very popular game with big people and little people alike. I'm not going to play dominoes with you this morning, but instead, I want to show you something that people have been doing with dominoes for years. [*Set up the dominoes and then give the first one a touch and watch them all fall in order.*] Isn't that interesting? You just touch one in front and all of them fall down.

Let me tell you why we did that little experiment. Jesus was talking the the disciples one day. He told them that people are a little bit like dominoes. This is expecially true when God is involved. Let's set up the dominoes again and we will call one of the dominoes "people," one of them you, one of them Jesus, and one of them God the Father. Jesus said that when people welcome you they are also welcoming Jesus, and God the Father. That means that when you are invited into someone's house he is also inviting Jesus and the Heavenly Father. When you touch one of the dominoes, you touch them all. The same thing happens when people do not invite you or welcome you into their homes. If they do not allow you to come, they are also cloing the door to Jesus and the Father. That is very interesting, isn't it.

Jesus was trying to tell the disciples how important it was that they knew that they were carrying the message of God. Wherever you go, you go in the name of Jesus. That is important. If people know that you are bringing the love of Jesus, then they will welcome you. You must never forget that. Just think, you are like a salesman for God. People will know what God is like through you. That is a very important thing to remember.

The next time you see a domino you will remember how you are very close to God, and what you do and say reflects on God in the eyes of other people.

PRACTICE!

Luke 10:25-37, vs. 37b: Then Jesus said, "Yes, now go and do the same."

Object: A baseball bat and a man dressed as a baseball coach to do some instructing.

Good morning, boys and girls. Today we have a special treat. Some of you may think that this is just for the boys, but it isn't. There are many girls playing this game now just like the boys. I have invited the best baseball coach I know to show all of the young people how to use a baseball bat. There are a lot of things to know about batting if you want to be a good hitter. I have brought a bat and I have asked Mr. Jones, the old expert baseball coach, to show us how to do it. [*Allow Mr. Jones to demonstrate how to hold the bat and how to stand and stride into the ball and things like that to give the right impression.*] That was very good, Mr. Jones, and I am sure that everyone who likes baseball learned a lot this morning.

Mr Jones is a good example. He showed us how to swing a bat correctly. Now what must you do if you want to be a good batter? [*Let them answer.*] That's right, you must practice what you have learned from Mr. Jones' example. It is the same way with our Christian faith. A lot of people listen to the answers and watch other people live the Christian life, but they don't practice it themselves. You need to practice it. You need to practice it a lot. That is what makes the difference.

Jesus told a story about a man who was a good example as a follower of God. When he finished telling the story about this man whom we call the good Samaritan, he told all the people who were listening that they should go out and try to do the same as the man in the story did.

Do you know a man or woman who is a practicing Christian? Is he doing a good job of it? Would you like to be like him? If you would, then you must practice doing it just as you would practice swinging a bat or anything else that you want to do well. Pick out the right example and then practice again and again. That way we get better at whatever we do. Pick out a practicing Christian and follow his example, and you will be a better Christian.

Will you try to do that? That's great.

GOOD TIMES

Luke 10:38-42, vs. 38: Her sister Mary sat on the floor, listening to Jesus as He talked.

Object: A kite, a stick, and a pocket knife.

Good morning, boys and girls. How many of you really enjoy the summer and all of the things that go with it? It's just great, isn't it? What do you like to do best? [*Have a couple of them answer your question.*] I have some things that I love to do that I have liked doing ever since I was a boy. How many of you like to fly kites? I just love it. Do you know why I like it? What do you think I learn and get out of flying kites? [*Let them answer.*] Those are some pretty good answers. I have something else that I would like to show you. [*Take out the knife and stick.*] How many of you have ever done this? [*Start to whittle.*] A lot of you! What do you learn, or get out of whittling? [*Let them answer.*] Those are good answers. I think though, that what I am going to say will surprise you. The reason I fly kites and whittle on wood is because it is fun. I don't really learn anything from doing it, but I do it simply because I love doing it, and it's fun.

Sometimes that's the way life is supposed to be, just fun. I remember a story about Jesus and his friends, Mary and Martha. Mary would always take the time to sit and enjoy Jesus while her sister Martha would work hard to make sure that everything was just right for Jesus. By the time Martha got around to being with Jesus, she was all tired out. Mary, on the other hand, enjoyed Jesus every moment. I think that Martha probably got a little angry with Mary because it seemed that she had to do all of the work. But Jesus told Martha that life was meant to be enjoyed and that he was meant to be enjoyed.

That is a very good lesson to learn about living and about Jesus. Some things are hard work and there is no other way to do them. But a lot of times are good times and should not be made anything else. Mary knew how to enjoy Jesus. I hope that many of you will remember that today when you go home and do something that you enjoy doing. Fly a kit, play a game or whittle a stick. All of these are things that Jesus would just love to do, and while he did it he would love every moment of it.

How many of you will try hard to enjoy what you are doing, just as Jesus wanted Martha to do? Raise your hands. That's wonderful.

ASK AND ASK AND ASK

Luke 11:1-13, vs. 9a: And so it is with prayer — keep on asking and you will keep on getting.

Object: A picnic basket.

Good morning, boys and girls. Does this sound familiar? "Mom let's go to the park for a picnic." "Mom, when are we going to go to the park for a picnic?" "Dad, will you play ball with me when we go to the park for our picnic?" "Mom, I hope that we are going to have hot dogs at the picnic." How many of you ever talk like this to your moms and dads? [*Wait for a show of hands.*] A lot of you. When you want to do something really special do you ask and ask and ask? Of course you do. It sounds a little bit like nagging, doesn't it, but there must be some kind of difference. Picnics are fun for the whole family, and moms and dads like things that are good for the family. It is different when you keep asking for bubblegum, another toy, or to stay up later at night than you should. Those things are not good for you, and your parents must say no many times as you ask. But when it is good for you and for everyone in the family, it is good that you ask and keep asking. That is what Jesus taught us to do with our Heavenly Father. Jesus taught us to keep right on asking for what we need and that God will give it to us.

[*Use the picnic basket.*] Whenever I see a picnic basket I think of all the times that someone has begged to go on a picnic. For moms and dads it seems like a lot of work and it takes a lot of planning. I guess that this is the reason it seems that they are so slow in getting ready.

I know big people who feel the same way about God. They ask and ask and ask before God does something for them. They wonder why it takes God so long to do something they know he can do in a flash. But God knows the best time and the best way to do it. He wants us to really appreciate it. When we ask and ask and ask then we also remember whom we asked, and where it is coming from.

The next time you go on a picnic and you have to ask your mom and dad a bunch of questions before you go, perhaps you will be reminded that it is often the same way when you pray to God. You may have to ask for what you need a hundred times, but if it is important enough to ask that often, you can be sure that God will give you an answer.

ENJOY WHAT YOU'VE GOT

Luke 12:13-21, vs. 15: Beware! Don't always be wishing for what you don't have. For real life and real living are not related to how rich we are.

Object: A bicycle and a lawn mower.

Good morning, boys and girls. I want to tell you a story today that I hope will teach you something the same way Jesus taught people a long time ago. The story is about a boy who loved to ride his bicycle and dream about being rich. He had the best time just riding around and looking at all of the fancy houses with their huge yards of green grass. In some of the yards there was a swimming pool with fancy chairs and tables around the pool. This boy would dream about how he would some day live in a big house, play in a huge yard and swim in a beautiful pool. Then one day the most amazing thing happened. The dream came true. His father told him about the big house that he bought with a big yard and a swimming pool. The boy was overjoyed and he could not wait until he moved into his new house. Every day he would get on his bike and just ride back and forth in front of this wonderful new house. But if you saw that boy today you would not think that he was the happy boy who dreamed of living in a big house with a big yard and a beautiful swimming pool. He is not happy anymore. If you drive by his house you will not see him riding his bike, but instead he is pushing a lawnmower. His yard is so big that he doesn't have time to ride his bike or play ball or visit with his friends. He cuts the grass, cleans the swimming pool and takes care of his big bedroom.

It's not a new story. Jesus told it a long time ago about people who were always wishing for something they didn't have. People who dream of being rich forget that this is not what counts here on earth. God promises us that it will be a lot better in heaven than even the richest man has life here on earth. But while we are on earth God wants us to enjoy the good things about living. When you have a lot of things you have to care for a lot of things, and it doesn't give much time to enjoy each other, the weather, and the other things like riding or flying a kite.

That's why Jesus told us not to wish for things that we don't have, but instead enjoy the things that are already given to us. I know that my friend who pushes a lawn mower all day wishes that he hadn't wished so much, so that he could go back to riding his bike. I hope you won't always be spending your time wishing for things you don't have, but rather be happy for the things that Jesus has given you.

GOD DOESN'T RUST

Luke 12:32-40, vs. 34: *Wherever your treasure is, there your heart and thoughts will also be.*

Object: *A girl's picture, a bank book, a car key.*

Good morning, boys and girls. How many of you have ever thought about finding a treasure in your heart? It seems like a funny place to find it, but a lot of people think that their treasure is in their heart. How many of you know what treasure is? [*Let them answer.*] That's right, it could be gold or silver or precious stones like diamonds. But the kind of treasure I am talking about may be riches, and may not be riches. For instance, some people consider the most important thing they have to be their bank book. [*Show the bank book.*] When you ask them what is the most important thing in the world to them they will tell you that it is the money they have in the bank. Other people might tell you it's the brand new car in the driveway. [*Hold up key to car.*] Still others think that the most important thing in the world is their girl friend. [*Hold up the picture.*] She is y far he most important and that man would rather be with her than anyone else. She is his treasure, and sometimes he is her treasure. The Bible teaches us that whatever is the most important thing to us is our treasure, and we will think about our treasure more than anything else.

Jesus teaches us that the kinds of things I have mentioned should not be the most important things in the world to us. Our feelings for God should come first. God is our treasure and when we put God first, we will think right about the other things. You can lose all of your money. It might be stolen or spent foolishly. You might wreck your car, or it may grow old and rusty. Your girl friend may find someone she likes better, or she may move away.

Everything in this world can be stolen, broken, or rusted away. People's feelings change. But God doesn't change or rust, and he can't be stolen or broken. That is why Jesus asks us to put God first and all other things second. Fill your heart with God and your heard will be filled with joy and never with disappointment. Perhaps you can think about what you call your treasure, and then you can see if God is first in your heart. I know that God wants to be first with you. How many of you will let God be first? Raise your hands. That's wonderful.

WHAT'S MISSING?

Luke 13:22-30, vss. 24-25: "The door to heaven is narrow. Work hard to get in, for the truth is that many will try to enter but when the head of the house has locked the door it will be too late. Then if you stand outside knocking, and pleading, 'Lord, open the door for us,' he will reply, 'I do not know you.' "

Object: A letter without a stamp, a billfold without money, and a comb without teeth.

Good morning, boys and girls. Today I have some riddles for you. They aren't very hard, but they will help to tell us something about what Jesus was teaching a long time ago. First of all, I have a letter with me but you have to tell me what is missing. [*Let them answer.*] That's right, a stamp. You can't mail a letter without a stamp. Let's look at an easy one. [*Hold up the comb.*] What is missing here? Right again. There are no teeth in the comb. You have a hard time combing hair with a comb that has no teeth. Let's try one more. [*Show them the billfold.*] What is missing from my billfold? Right again. There isn't any money. Things do make a difference. Stamps, teeth in a comb, and money are all things that make a difference if you want letters, combed hair and billfolds to do their jobs.

The same thing is true about heaven, according to Jesus. If you want to be a citizen in heaven then you must follow the teachings of God. Jesus tells us that it is important to try to be what God expects and to do what you know is right. Some people think that they can be a follower of Jesus later, whenever they want. Jesus says that this is not true. We become a part of his people when he asks us to be a part, and not when we feel like it. That is a big difference. We may wait around and it will be too late. We will be like a letter without a stamp, or a comb without teeth. We may want to get to heaven very much, but we are like the man who wants to buy a gift and has no money in his billfold. No money, no gift. That's the way it is.

Jesus says that we must be ready for God's invitation to become part of his heaven and not wait till we think the time is right for us. The next time you see a letter I hope that you look for the stamp. Check your comb to see that it has all of its teeth and keep your money in the billfold. Then you will remember that you must be ready for God to invite you to be part of his heaven. I hope you will all do that.

FRIEDA AND FRED

Luke 14:1, 7-14, vs. 11: For everyone who tries to honor himself shall be humbled; and he who humbles himself shall be honored.

Object: Some sterling silver and some everyday stainless tableware.

Good morning, boys and girls. I want to tell you a story about a friend of mine who I think will help you to understand another one of Jesus' teachings. This is the story about a couple of friends called Frieda and Fred Fork. They looked a lot alike but they were as different as night and day. I can show you what my friends look like and maybe you can tell the difference. [*Show them the piece of sterling silverware (Frieda) and the piece of stainless (Fred).*] How many of you can see the difference? [*Let them answer.*] Both of them are used for eating, or at least that is the way the people who made them intended both of them to be used. However, I heard Frieda say one day to one of her very snobbish friends Sylvia Spoon that she would never be caught in anyone's mouth. She was too good for that. People were made to look at her and not to touch. She bruised easily. Frieda just loved to have someone polish and shine her and then lay her gently back on the table where people could pass by and admire her. Frieda thought a lot of herself and she didn't mind anyone knowing it.

Now Fred is a lot different. He doesn't mind being used to eat with, and as a matter of fact he rather enjoys it. I don't think there is anything that makes him happier than when a young boy or girl first learns to use him. He's not fussy about the way he is kept clean. A little soap and water are fine. It feels good to be dried by a fluffy towel but he doesn't mind just laying in the dish drainer drying with the other dishes and silverware. That is the great part about being a Fred. He knows what he is and he likes being used. I like him too and I use him every day. I guess Fred likes being the way he is also because he is out every day enjoying life with the family and all of his friends. But poor Frieda — she moans and groans all of the time because she is kept in a dark box, covered up with hot cloth. It can't be much fun just being pretty when there are so very few times even to be seen.

I think that is what Jesus was talking about when he said that people who think too much about themselves are usually not well liked and people who seldom think of themselves are always thinking of others and looking for new ways to be used are thought a lot of. Some people like to brag, Jesus told us, and they have little place in God's world. But the people who do not brag, but do good because it is right are the ones who will share heaven with him. Do you want to share heaven with God? That's good, because that's what God wants for you.

WHICH COMES FIRST?

Luke 14:25-33, vs. 33: So no one can become my disciple unless he first sits down and counts his blessings and then renounces them all for me.

Object: Two boxes. In one box you have a house key, driver's license, money, diploma, wedding ring. In the other box you have only a picture of Jesus.

Good morning, boys and girls. Today I have brought with me a couple of boxes that I thought you might be interested in. I don't think anyone is really too interested in the boxes themselves, but I know that most people love to know what is kept inside of boxes. One box is worth a lot more than the other. Jesus told us that we must first know what is in one box before we can really know how valuable the other one is to us.

I am going to show you one box, and you must think about how valuable it could be to you, and if you would like to have the things that belong to the person who has this box. [*Open the box with all of the items and pull them out one at a time.*] First, I have a key, a very important key that opens a special door. Would you like to guess what this key is for? [*Let them answer.*] It is the key to the front door of a house. Next, I have a license. What do people have licenses for? That's right, a car, and that is what this is. A driver's license which means that the person who owns this box has a car. It could be a shiny new one. Then we have money, lots of money, which means that the person who owns this box is rich. There is also a diploma. This means that this person has had a fine education. Here is a diamond ring, which means that this person is married and perhaps has a family. I would say that the person who owns this box has everything. It looks like a very valuable box to me. Do you think that this is the most valuable box or do you think that it is the other one? [*Let them answer.*] Let's open the other box and see what is inside. Does anyone have a guess before we open it? Those are pretty good guesses but let's see for ourselves. [*Open the second box.*]

It's a picture of Jesus. I wonder which one of these I would take if I had the chance. The picture of Jesus means that the person who has this box thinks that Jesus is valuable and important and he is a follower of the Master. Would you give up all of the things in the other box to be a follower of Jesus? It is a pretty hard decision, but one that we all have to make. Which comes first, Jesus or houses, cars, money, diplomas, and families? Jesus says that we should count all of our blessings. That is what all of these things are. Then we should choose him first, and put all of the other things second. That is a big choice, but it is the exact one that Jesus asks us to make. I wonder which one you will choose. I know which one you should choose.

HE MAKES THE BAD GOOD

1 Timothy 1:12-17, vs. 16: But God had mercy on me so that Christ Jesus could use me as an example to show everyone how patient he is with even the worst sinners, so that others will realize that they, too, can have everlasting life.

Object: A good exåmple such as a picture that shows a person before and after he has lost weight or before and after he has added muscle.

Good morning, boys and girls. How many of you have ever looked through a magazine or a newspaper? Almost all of you. Have you ever seen something like this? [*Show them the ads.*] What does it mean when you see a picture of a very fat person in one picture, and a not-so-fat person in the next picture? [*Let them answer.*] That's right, it means that she has lost weight. How about this one that shows a very skinny man in one picture and then a very strong looking man with lots of muscles in the other. Do you know what that means? That's right. It means that the man has built his body with exercise and great effort. These are what we call examples, good examples. The people who have accomplished what is shown in these pictures feel good because they know that they look better now than they did before. Not only that, but they feel that they are good examples for other people and others will feel better if they work hard at being like them.

Paul felt that he was an example. It was a lot different from the pictures that I have shown you. Paul was not an example of how a man looked with new muscles or how a person would feel if he lost a lot of weight. Paul thought that God had chosen him as an example of how a bad man could be made into a good man by knowing Jesus. Paul told everyone how he had tried to hurt the church and the Christians who followed

Jesus. He was a bad man. But God wanted Paul to work for him. In spite of all the bad things he did, God forgave him for his sins and asked Paul to work for him.

Just think about how God can make a bad man into a good man. It is a good example for all of us. Some people feel that they are not good enough to work for God and to be near God. But Paul said he is a good example of how God will care for the worst sinner and bring him into the church.

Maybe the next time you see one of these pictures in the paper you will think about Paul and how God used this bad man and made him a good man to tell everyone about the love of Jesus.

A REAL CHOICE

Luke 16:1-13, vs. 13: "For neither you nor anyone else can serve two masters. You will hate one and show loyalty to the other, or else the other way around, you will be enthusiastic about one and despise the other. You cannot serve both God and money."

Object: Two ball caps that represent two different teams.

Good morning, boys and girls. This is a real day of decision. I must do something about a very big problem I have made for myself, and I want you to help me if you will. I have been playing baseball for two teams this whole season and I have had a lot of fun, but now I have a real problem. The two teams are going to play each other and I don't know which team to play for in the game. First of all, there is the red team. They have bright and beautiful uniforms and they let me play first base. I just love to play first base for the red team. But then there is the blue team. It is a great team, too, and I pitch for the blue team. There is nothing like standing out there with the ball in your hand and waiting for the batter to come up so you can strike him out.

I wish I could play first base for the red team and pitch for the blue team in the game, but then it would be my turn to bat and I couldn't pitch the ball, run and get a bat in time to hit it. And if I could, what would happen if somebody threw the ball to first base and I wasn't there to catch it? Do you see what I mean? It is very confusing. You can't play for two teams because you can't do your best for both teams. You will want one team or the other to win. It is very complicated. I must decide on one team. What do you think? [*Let them answer.*] It helped me to tell you my problem, and now I know that I cannot play ball for two teams. I must choose one of them.

That is the kind of advice that Jesus gave us about the choice we have with our life. Some people live only for the good times they can have today. They want all of the money they can get and all of the things that money can buy. They think that God is important, but maybe he is not so important right now. Jesus says that we must make a choice now between God and money. We can't wait till later. Jesus says we are either on God's team, or on the other team, and we cannot be on both. That is a real choice. We all have to make it and tell ourselves which is the most important. You will have to make that choice, too, and God is always waiting to hear which one you make.

GOD FIRST

Luke 16:1-13, vs. 10: No! For unless you are honest in small matters, you won't be honest in large ones. If you cheat even a little, you won't be honest with greater responsibilities.

Object: A large box filled with heavy books.

Good morning, boys and girls. I have a little experiment that I would like to try out on you. I wonder if some of you would be willing to do a little hard work and serve as volunteers. You would? Very good. This is our problem. I have this very heavy box of books that I want moved from where it is to the other side of the church. [*Point to where you want them moved.*] Now, I have tried to move the box and I haven't been too successful because I have a sore back. I want you to understand that I am strong enough to move them, but I just don't know how my back would be if I tried to lift all of those books. Is there anyone strong enough to lift the books over there? [*Wait for volunteers.*] Very good. Now just try to move the books without dragging the box on the floor, because I don't want the floor scratched. [*Let them try to lift it.*] That is a tough one, isn't it? What are we going to do? I must get the books over to the other place. [*Let them think with you.*] Do you think a girl might be able to do it? I know some very strong girls.

I knew that this was a tough job. I didn't really think that anyone here could move the books, but even with my bad back I know how to do it. Do you think there might be any other way to get the books over to the other side of the church without lifting that heavy box. [*Let them answer.*] How about this way? [*Take one book out of the box and carry it to the other side of the church.*] That's the way to do it. Sometimes we have to learn how to do things in a small way before we can do them in a big way.

It is the same way with other things. Some people just know that they could solve all of their problems if they had a million dollars. They think that money is the answer. God doesn't think so. When you have one dollar you have one problem. When you have a million dollars you have a million problems. God tells us that we cannot worry and take care of big problems until we can take care of small problems. First things must come first. Before we can worry about money, we must first know that everything is right with God. God comes before money. When we are right with God and do what he teaches, then we can use our money in the right way and it will not give us any problems. It is like moving books. If you try to move the whole box you are like a man who has a million dollars and doesn't know what to do with it. When you move them one at a time then that is like putting God first because you have solved your problem.

God teaches us that we must work with him first before we work with money, power or anything else. God is first and everything else is second. Will you try to remember that God is first? That's what God wants you to do.

PAY ATTENTION

Luke 16:19-31, vs. 31: But Abraham said, "If they won't listen to Moses and the prophets, they won't listen even though someone rises from the dead."

Object: A "WET PAINT" sign, a freshly painted board with a fingerprint or two showing clearly on it.

Good morning, boys and girls. How many of you listen carefully when you are told how to do something? [*Let them raise their hands.*] That's good, very good. Not everyone is like you. I want to show you something. [*Take out the board.*] Do you see this board? Would you believe that this board was just painted? Do you see anything wrong with it? [*Let them answer.*] I have something else to show you. See this sign? What does the sign say? [*Let them read it.*] Do you know now what is wrong? You are right. I painted this board and put up the sign and someone put his fingers on the board after he read the sign. I don't think the sign did any good. What do you think? Of course, I also know that a lot of people passed my painted board and only one or two touched it. That must mean that a lot of people read the sign and stayed away from the board, and a few read the sign and touched it.

I want to explain to you the reason why I did this. A lot of people have read the Bible and know that there is a way for them to live according to God's teachings. A lot of people who read it think about what it says, and they try to live the way God wants them to live. Those are the same people who read my sign, *"WET PAINT"* and left it alone. There are some other people who read what God says, and do just the opposite. Those are the people who have read my sign and still put their hands on the board. You can often tell who the people are who have touched the sign, because they have red paint on their hands. It is not that way with the people who have read the Bible and who do as God says.

There will be a time when it will make a real difference. Those who listen to God and pay attention to what they hear will live with him forever, and they will love being with him. But those who read the Bible and don't pay any attention are not going to live with God, and they will be sorry for it. That's what Jesus taught his followers. I hope that you pay as much attention to God's Word as you said you would to my sign. Then you will live forever with God and be happy as you can be.

FAITH IS STRONG

Luke 17:1-10, vs. 6: "If your faith were only the size of a mustard seed," Jesus answered, "it would be large enough to uproot that mulberry tree over there and send it hurtling into the sea! Your command would bring immediate results!"

Object: A board that acts as a lever and something fairly heavy that children would have a hard time lifting.

Good morning, boys and girls. Today we are going to learn how a little bit of something that we call faith can be stronger than anything else that we know. First of all I must tell you that Jesus told us that faith is the most powerful thing in the world. Faith is believing in something that we cannot see, but that we know is there. We have faith in God. We cannot see God, but we believe that he is here and everywhere. Faith, Jesus said, is like a mustard seed. A mustard seed is very small, but it grows into one of the biggest plants. If you only have a little faith you can do wonderful things. Let me show you what I mean.

Do you remember a couple of weeks ago when I asked you to get a box of books to the other side of the room? Do you remember that the box was too heavy and we had to carry a book at a time? If you remember that, then you will think that I am trying to trick you again, but I am not. I have a very heavy box and I want you to be able to lift it and move it across the room. I really want you to do this. I know that this box weighs more than the book box did, but I am sure that you can move it. This is show. I have a piece of wood that I am going to call faith, and I am going to put it under the box. Let's lean on the box until it is tilted and then we will slip the wood called faith under it. [Do it as we have described.] Now you could not lift this box or hold it up as we are going to do for very long without the piece of wood called faith. But with this piece of wood we can lift it or lower it or just hold it for almost as long as we want to. It is not as big as the box, and it doesn't weigh nearly as much as the box, but it will do the job for almost as long as we want to do it.

That is the way faith works. You don't need a lot of it, but the more you use it the more you will have of it. Faith is strong and it can do almost anything, according to Jesus. Remember what faith is, and use it. Faith is believing in a God that you cannot see, but who is everywhere and is always willing to help you. You can use faith when you are sick, or well, rich or poor, young or old. Faith comes from God, and it is the best help for every problem there is in the whole world. How many of you have faith? That's great and I hope you will never lose it.

SIN'S PULL

John 8:31-36, vs. 32: Jesus said to them, "You are truly my disciples if you live as I tell you to, and you will know the truth, and the truth will set you free."

Object: A piece of rope that you can tie to one of the children's wrists.

Good morning, boys and girls. How many of you have ever thought that you could be a slave? Not many of you. Jesus thinks that you could be a slave, and as a matter of fact, if you are not a believer in Jesus, he thinks that you are a slave. Now a slave belongs to someone doesn't he? Who do you think that you might belong to if you are not a follower of Jesus? [*Let them answer.*] The devil is a good answer. Jesus says that you can be a slave to sin. That is almost like the devil. I wonder if you know what it would be like to be a slave. A slave cannot think or act for himself. A slave must always do what the master says he should do.

Let's try a little experiment. I am going to tie a rope around your arm and make your arm my slave. I won't hurt you, but we are going to pretend that your arm is my slave. Now while I am talking to the rest of the people, we will see what my slave does. [*Go on and talk about the terrible part of being a slave to sin and all of the time you are doing this, play and tug on the rope.*] It would be awful to be a slave as your arm is to my rope. The only time that you can move your arm is when I pull the rope. Jesus said that this is the way that some people are to sin. The only time that they act, is when their sin tells them to. It is awful.

But Jesus said there is another way, and he hopes that we will try it. If we begin to follow Jesus we will be free from sin and trouble. We can be ourselves and no one will be able to hurt us. That is the best part of being a follower of Jesus. We are free. Imagine what it would be like to have a rope around you all of your life and then have it taken off. Do you know what you would feel like? You would feel wonderful. That is the way that God wants you to feel. Get rid of your sin by telling Jesus what it is and you will feel like you got rid of a rope. Then follow Jesus and it will be like feeling free forever. That's the way a Christian wants it, and that is the way that God makes it.

JESUS IS A GOOD GOD

John 11:32-44, vs. 36: "They were close friends," the
Jewish leaders said. "See how much he loved him."

Object: An empty candy bar wrapper and one dime.

Good morning, boys and girls. How many of you
have a good friend? A lot of you have good friends,
and I think that is great. What makes a person a good
friend? [Let them answer.] It's kind of hard to say what
a good friend is, isn't it? I think you feel or just know a
good friend.

I brought along some things that I remember about a
good friend of mine. I remember the time that we were
walking home from school one day. I was so hungry
and I told my friend about it. Do you know what he did?
He reached in his lunch box and gave me his candy
bar. He didn't ask for part of it, or even if I wanted to
share it. He just gave me the whole thing. I remember
another time when I needed a dime and he gave me
the last dime he had so I would have enough money to
buy a birthday present for my mother. Both of those
things are hard to forget, but the one thing I will always
remember is the time I got hurt and the pain was just
awful. I thought that I was going to die and I was so
afraid. I remember looking at my friend and I shall
never forget it. He wasn't afraid and he wasn't hurt, but
he had some tears in his eyes because he knew how bad
I felt. That's a friend.

If you read the story that I read in the Bible today,
you will also know how good a friend Jesus can be. His
friend Lazarus had died and Jesus cried. Everyone
knew what good friends Jesus and Lazarus were, but
they never expected to see Jesus cry. Jesus cried, and
there were real tears in his eyes.

I want you to know that Jesus is someone who really
cares about his friends. He really cares about us, and he

hurts when we hurt, just as he laughs when we laugh. A lot of people think that Jesus only watches us because he wants to know if we go to church or if we do right or wrong. I don't think that this is the reason that Jesus cares about us at all. Jesus loves us and he is with us wherever we go. If we hurt, then he hurts, and if we are happy, then he is happy. Jesus is a good God and he not only loves us like God, but he also cares about us like a friend.

GOD KNOWS THE DIFFERENCE

Luke: 18:9-14, vs. 14: I tell you, this sinner, not the Pharisee, returned home forgiven! For the proud shall be humbled, but the humble shall be honored.

Object: Some guest hand towels and some everyday hand towels.

Good morning, boys and girls. I have a little puzzle for you today. I brought some towels with me and I want you to tell me which ones you think are my favorite ones. Now, take a very good look at these towels because it is important that you know when they are used and what they are called. First of all, I want to show you my ordinary towels. These towels are the ones I use every day, and I dry my hands on them after I have washed them with soap and water. I may have used them after working on the greasy engine of my car, or after cleaning up the yard. These towels are tough, and they have been used often.

On the other hand I have some very fancy towels that we get out when we are going to have company. They look beautiful. These are called guest towels. Do you see all of the fancy thread and the wonderful designs? Aren't they something? They wouldn't be the kind of thing that you would use after hard work, or if you had to rub anything very hard. These are really fancy towels, and they are very expensive.

Now which do you think are my favorite towels? That's right, the everyday towels. These towels remind me a lot of people. Some people are so fancy that you know that you could never use them. They don't have the time and they are not interested in you. They wouldn't understand your problems because they would never want you to think that they knew what problems were all about. They are like the guest towels. They are just to be looked at. But the everyday towel is a real towel. It likes to be used just like real people. They want to help, and they can help because they have had problems just like you.

God knows the difference between real people just like you and fancy people, and I know the difference between towels. God knows when you are being pretend people. Some of us call people like that fancy towel a "fake" or a "hypocrite." God says that the fakes will be found out and put down, but the real people, like the real towels, will not only be used but will also be honored.

The reason that I tell you this is so that you will know how much God really cares that we are real people and not fakes. He doesn't want us to pretend to each other or to him. He wants us to be real and to be used to help and serve each other and him. God knows the difference and God knows us.

THE LITTLE SHORT MAN

Luke 19:1-10, vs. 4: So he ran ahead and climbed into a sycamore tree beside the road to watch from there.

Object: Some binoculars.

Good morning, boys and girls. How many of you have ever been to a football game in a big stadium? Have you ever been near the top of the stadium so that when you looked out at the field where the football players were playing they looked like ants? They are really far away when they look like this. What do you do when you are this far away from something that you really want to see? I know what I do, and I am going to share it with you. I take a pair of binoculars with me. [*Show them the binoculars.*] Do you know what happens when I use these funny looking glasses? [*Let them answer.*] That's right, everything looks closer. The players can come so close through these special glasses that you can see their faces and hands. It is a wonderful way to watch anything that is far away.

I remember a story about a man who was too short to see Jesus, and he wanted to see him so much. Do you know what he did? He climbed a tree, and instead of trying to look between the legs of the other people, he got closer than anyone by lying down on the tree limb so that he would not miss Jesus when he passed by. Jesus looked up and saw him and asked if he could spend part of the day at this short man's house. The little man was thrilled! He could hardly wait to tell his friends and neighbors about his wonderful guest.

I suppose you know who I am talking about. Everyone has heard about the short man who climbed up into a tree to see Jesus. Can you tell me his name? [*Let them answer.*] Zacchaeus, right. But there is something about Zacchaeus that very few people know. They know that he was short and that he climbed a tree and that Jesus ate and visited at his house, but did you know that Zacchaeus told Jesus about all of the terrible things that he had done, and that he promised to make it up to all the people he had hurt?

Jesus knew what kind of man this little short man another chance. Jesus was ready to forgive his sins and let him start all over. Some people forget that Jesus is a friend to people who do wrong, and that he is ready to give them another chance if they are ready to try again. Zacchaeus may have been short, but he had a lot of courage and trusted Jesus to help him do right.

How many of you will trust Jesus to give you another chance? Remember, Jesus always wants to give you a chance to do better.

SIGN OF THE KING

Luke 23:35-43, vs. 38: A signboard was nailed to the cross above him with these words: "This is the King of the Jews."

Object: Nameplates with the words "manager," "pastor," "doctor" on them. Then one sign with the words written on it "This is the King of the Jews."

Good morning, boys and girls. Today we are going to play a very simple game, and I want to see if you can catch on to it. A lot of times you will go places and see signs like I am going to show you. I want you to tell me what the sign says and what you think you will find behind the door that has the sign on it.

[*Hold up nameplate with Doctor written on it.*] What does it say? That's right, and what does the sign mean if you see it on a door? Very good. It means that behind that door there is a man or a woman who takes care of people when they are sick or keeps them from getting sick. Let's try another one. [*Use the one with Pastor written on it.*] That's right, it says Pastor, but what does it means? It means that behind that door there is a man who teaches about Jesus and takes care of people who want to know Jesus better. Here is one more. [*The word is Manager.*] A manager. What does a manager do? [*Let them answer.*] He could do a lot of things like take care of a store or an apartment house or a factory. It usually means that he is in charge wherever he works.

Now I want you to look at one more sign, and I am going to read it to you very carefully. [*Hold up the sign that says, "This is the King of the Jews."*] Do you know who this sign was written for and what it means? That's right, it was written for Jesus, but do you know who wrote it? [*Let them answer.*] People who were his enemies wrote it because they thought that they were making fun of Jesus and the Jews. But how wrong they were. Jesus was a different kind of King than the kind they had always known before. Jesus was a King of all people and not of any one group. Jesus is a King because he is the ruler of us all. He forgives sin, he cares for people who are hurt and hungry. Jesus is the King of the rich, the poor, the ugly and the good-looking.

Jesus is the King of the whole world. They were right when they made a sign and called him a King, but they didn't know what the sign that they made really meant. I want you to remember this sign that men wrote about Jesus. I hope that you never forget it. This sign tells more about Jesus than all of the Doctor, Pastor or Manager signs that you will ever see. Just think, Jesus hanging on the cross and dying is called a King. He is the King, the King of the whole world.

BE ALERT!

Matthew 24:37-44, vss. 43 & 44: Just as a man can prevent trouble from thieves by keeping watch for them, so you can avoid trouble by always being ready for my unannounced return.

Object: A pair of binoculars and a sailor's hat.

Good morning, boys and girls. Can you tell me who wears a hat like this? How many of you have ever watched a movie where a sailor, wearing a hat like this, is keeping watch from a very high pole? Do you remember what he did while he was up there? [*Let them answer.*] That's right, he looked one way and then the other way, and if he saw anything that was strange, he would shout to the captain and tell him the direction to look. Today a sailor would have a pair of very powerful binoculars if he were on a small ship, or he would watch a radar screen if he were on a larger ship. He would always look for the unexpected. It might be a ship, or a storm, or a piece of land that the sailor keeping watch might see. But whatever it is, he must warn the captain so that he can avoid any trouble.

Jesus has asked us to keep the same kind of watch for him that a sailor would keep on a ship. Jesus wants to make sure that we will not miss him when he comes back to greet us. You can imagine how you would feel if you told everyone to look for you and then no one showed up when you arrived. Jesus wants to make sure that this does not happen. He asked that everyone be prepared to meet him.

How do you prepare for Jesus? I don't think that we will see Jesus on a radar screen or with some high powered binoculars. Jesus says that he will be seen by all of the people who believe in him and live the way he taught us to live. That means that we could have the most powerful radar system in the world and we would not be able to see Jesus if we were not followers of his. He is only coming back to the people who have followed him. Other people will not be able to greet him and to see him. That is why it is so important for us to follow his teachings and be ready for Jesus to come back.

A sailor could allow a ship to run into an iceberg if he did not keep a steady watch. If he fell asleep on the job for only a few minutes, the ship could be wrecked. If he only watched on one side of the ship, he might miss someone on the other side in a life raft who was hoping to be saved. A sailor must be alert at all times. So must a Christian who is waiting for Jesus to come back to earth as he promised he would. He must be alert and ready to welcome Jesus into his heart.

How many of you think you will be alert and ready? **Wonderful!**

PEANUTS IN THE SHELL

Matthew 3:1-12, vs. 12: He will separate the chaff from the grain, burning the chaff with never-ending fire, and storing away the grain.

Object: Peanuts in the shell.

Good morning, boys and girls. How many of you like peanuts? Almost all of you. That's good. There are two parts to the peanut when you buy them this way. [*Hold up some peanuts.*] There is the shell which you can see, and inside is the nut which we call the peanut. I know some people who eat the whole peanut, shell and all. But very few people do that. Most of us crack the peanut shell, open it, and then take out the nut and eat it. But what do we do with the shell? We don't eat it. You can't make anything else out of a peanut shell, so what do you do with it? Right. You throw it away. You burn it, or maybe you bury it, but you don't use it.

Jesus compared people in the same way. He said that some people are believers, and they love God. They believe that God will take care of them, and that he will build a place for them to live forever. But what about the people who do not love him and do not follow his teachings? Jesus says that they shall be gotten rid of in the same way that we get rid of peanut shells.

One of the reasons that Jesus is coming back to earth is to tell those who are like the peanuts that they are loved by God, and that they will have a place with him forever. He will also tell the people who have despised God that they do not have a place in God's Kingdom. That sounds kind of bad for the people who do not love God, but that is the way Jesus says it is going to be.

Jesus came to earth the first time so that we would know what God expects of us, and what we are to believe. He told us then that all we had to do was to trust and believe in him and that we would live forever. All of us hope that we will be like the peanut inside of the shell and not like the shell itself. The peanut is saved and has a place with God. The shell is burned or buried.

Jesus knows who loves and trusts in him and shares his love with others. Those are the people who will live with God forever in peace. God's people are like the peanuts inside the shells and others who are filled with hate and do not believe are like the shells that are burned or buried.

I hope you will all try to be like the inside of the peanut.

THE RIGHT KEY

Matthew 11:2-11, vs. 3: "Are you really the one we are waiting for, or shall we keep on looking?"

Object: Some keys on a key ring and a lock that is opened by one of them.

Good morning, boys and girls. I have a small problem today. I am sure that you have had the same problem, or you have watched your father and mother have the problem. The problem is not so bad today, because I have plenty of light and I can see what I am doing. But every once in a while I am somewhere in the dark and I have to open a door and I don't know what key it is that fits the lock. There I am taking each key and trying the lock in the dark. It is hard enough to find the key hole, but then when you can't find the key and you have to keep trying each key until you find one that fits, it is real trouble. [*Keep trying different keys. The more keys you have, the better the story.*]

That is the way that some people felt about Jesus. They had heard that Jesus was the Savior, and they wanted him to be the Savior, but they were not quite sure. There had been other people who had said that they were sent from God, and some of them pretended pretty well. The people were kind of confused. One day a group of men who had been with John the Baptizer came to Jesus and asked him if he were the Son of God, the Savior, or should they keep on looking for someone else. It is kind of like a key that looks like it should fit, but you have tried so many that look just like it you are not sure if it will work. They asked Jesus that question and he told them the true answer. He said that he did everything the prophets had said the Savior would do, and he believed he was the Savior, so they could decide for themselves. That is the best answer that he could give.

It is the same answer for all of us today. Some people wonder if it is true that Jesus is the Son of God and the Savior of the world. He had done everything that God said he should do, and all of us have to decide for ourselves.

It is just like this key. It looks to me like it is the one for this lock. There is only one way that I am going to know for sure. I will have to try it for myself. If it fits and opens the lock, then it must be the right key for the lock. If it is not the right key, then I will have to look for another. I think that this key is the same that Jesus is for me. I think that it is the right one [*Try the key.*] It is the right one for this lock! Jesus is the Savior of the world! If anyone you know has asked if Jesus is the Savior, you can tell them for me that Jesus is the Son of God and they do not have to look for anyone else.

THE RIGHT ANSWER

Matthew 1:18-25, vs. 21: And you will have a Son, and you shall name Him Jesus [meaning "Savior"], for He will save His people from their sins.

Object: An adding machine.

Good morning, boys and girls. How many of you like to add figures? I want someone who is really good at arithmetic to help me add some figures. Do I have a volunteer who is really good at adding? [*Choose someone from the group.*] This is a fine volunteer. Do you get A's in arithmetic?

Now I am going to give you some numbers and I want you to add them up and remember you are not allowed to make a mistake. Here are the numbers. 3, 5, 9, 16, 22. Do you have the answer? We must have an answer. I'll give them to you once more. 3, 5, 9, 16, 22. Do you have an answer this time? Does anyone have the answer? If you make a mistake, I will lose everything I have. I need the answer, and the right one if I am going to be perfect. I thought that you could help. Would you like to try one more time? Here they are: 3, 5, 9, 16, 22. I think that you just gave me the wrong answer. I have a better way and one that I am sure will not make a mistake. Let's try this adding machine and see what answer it gives us. [*Punch the numbers on the adding machine and total it.*] The answer is 55. Shall we give it a couple of additional problems and see how it does? The adding machine does not make a mistake.

Did you know that Jesus is like an adding machine for people instead of numbers? He is. Jesus saves us from our mistakes. We call our mistakes sins, and our sins cause us a lot of problems. But no matter how many sins we have made, Jesus is sure to save us if we trust in him. I know that I can trust my adding machine to save me from my adding mistakes. I know that it will not let me down and make some bad error. Jesus is like that with our sins. Jesus came to earth to save us from our mistakes. That is why he is called Jesus. Jesus means "Savior," and he saves us from our mistakes.

An adding machine is something that all of us have seen and we know we can trust because it always gives us the right answer. I can tell you that the same thing is true of Jesus. He never makes a mistake of his own, and he can save us from the ones we make. The next time you see an adding machine, you can think of Jesus and how his name means Savior, Jesus comes to save us from our sins.

WARNINGS

Matthew 2:13-15, 19-23, vs. 13: After they were gone, an angel of the Lord appeared to Joseph in a dream. "Get up and flee to Egypt with the baby and his mother," the angel said, "and stay there until I tell you to return for King Herod is going to try to kill the child.

Object: A flashlight with a blinking red light.

Good morning, boys and girls. How many of you know what I mean when I say the word "warning?" [*Let them answer.*] That's right, a warning is something you see or hear that keeps you from some danger. A warning can be a sign or a sound. A siren can be a warning. When you hear a siren you know that you must get out of the way so that the policeman or fireman can get to where he is going.

I have another warning. [*Hold up the blinking red flashlight.*] When you see a light blinking like that you know that there is danger and you should be careful. People do this when their car breaks down on the road and they want others to see the car and not run into it. Sometimes people will put up lights like this if there is a hole in the road. When you see that kind of a light, you know that it is a warning.

There are other kinds of warnings. I want to tell you about one that happened to Joseph, the earthly father of Jesus. He had a dream that told him to take Jesus and his mother and go to Egypt because the King of Israel was jealous of Jesus and that he would kill him. It was a warning, and Joseph knew enough about the ways God worked to believe what he had dreamed. Joseph could have thought about it and maybe talked about it to some of his friends, but he knew that he did not have time. If God told him in a dream to go, he would go. He knew that God would only warn him if he needed to be warned.

Joseph told Mary of his dream and they took the baby Jesus and left for Egypt where they waited until they heard from God that everything was all right.

Not all dreams are warnings, and not all flashlights are warnings, but when they are, we should watch and listen to them. Joseph had a warning, and it saved the life of Jesus while he was still a baby. The next time you see a red blinking flashlight, or any other kind of warning, you can remember the time that Joseph had a warning in a dream and he believed it. It helped to save Jesus' life so that he could do the work that God had promised he would do.